Dedicated to all the US Veterans who have served their nation.

Ed sitting on a B-24 Liberator Pratt & Whitney engine.

Edward William Wickemeyer

Right after the attack on Pearl Harbor in 1941, many recruiting centers popped up all over the United-States. One of these recruiting offices opened up in Ft. Thomas, Kentucky, just a couple of miles from where Edward William Wickemeyer lived in Dayton, Kentucky with his parents and his younger brother. On October 30, 1942 Ed and his best friend Robert Werry, also from Dayton, Kentucky, decided to head to that recruitment center in Fort Thomas and sign up for selective service training.

Soon after they enlisted they were off to Sedalia Army Airfield in Warrensburg, Missouri. Basic training taught them, along with specific skills, to think of themselves less as individuals and more as an integral part of a unit in a branch of the military. Although they enlisted together, Ed and Bob ended up in different branches of service. Bob found his way into the Navy and Ed went through more specialized training for specific duties in the newly evolved component of Army Air Corps, the United States Army Air Forces (USAAF). Ed, at the young age of 19, was soon to learn the basic skills of an airman including marching in formation, loading, unloading and cleaning weapons, along with more specialized training for specific duties such as parachuting, radio communications and operations, and the use of photographic equipment.

Ed trained for eighteen months and traveled to many different bases located within the United States before being deployed overseas. He spent ten months and thirteen days of foreign service in the Asiatic Pacific. During his foreign service and on most of his 40+ missions he carried a camera. As an amateur, he photographed many interesting images documenting his travels and experiences, many of which are shared in this book.

After spending a total of two years, seven months, and ten days serving his country, he returned to the States on June 9, 1945 arriving at Union Terminal in Cincinnati, Ohio. He was welcomed by his parents Ruth and William Wickemeyer and his OAO (one and only) Nancy McNamara. Two years later on June 21, 1947, he married Nancy and they began their journey together for the rest of their lives.

Ed's Journal Books

These two journals were recently discovered in the basement of Ed's wife, Nancy Wickemeyer's home in Newtown Ohio just outside of Cincinnati. The following pages contain the merging of these two journals based on the entry dates in the two books. Copy from the large journal, pictured on the left in the photo above, is indicated by the use of regular 12pt. Garamond type. The small journal on the right, "The Mission Book" is indicated in **bold type** and you will see the word **Mission** before each paragraph. We don't exactly know why there are two separate journals but we assume one remained at camp and the other was kept on the B24. There are also side notes in gray that explain in more detail the events happening in the journals.

Edward and Nancy's wedding June 21, 1947.

Edward Wickemeyer and best friend Robert Werry.

The Uninvited B-24

The B-24 Liberator is a long-range heavy bomber that could reach 290 miles per hour and carry a 5,000-pound bomb load for 1,700 miles. It had impressive speed and altitude abilities for its time. The B-24 was used extensively in the South Pacific, conducting bombing missions against Japanese-held islands, airfields, and Naval targets. Its long-range capabilities made it suitable for reaching and attacking targets across the vast expanse of the Pacific Ocean. The B-24 Liberator was first put into action in 1941, the production continued until 1945. A total of almost 19,000 B-24s were built during the war. Currently there are only two aircraft that are airworthy with six complete airplanes on static display in various museums . The surviving examples are now valuable historical artifacts, and efforts are being made to preserve and maintain them for future generations to appreciate.

Sergeants meeting next to The Uninvited.

● **"The Uninvited"**

Appropriately called, it was decorated with a pin-up girl holding a machine gun and its own emblem. Nose painting became a well-liked custom among aircrews. On the planes' noses, numerous patterns, names, pin-up girls, cartoon characters, and other customized motifs were painted. These decorations frequently served as a morale booster, identity builder, or tribute to loved ones or home towns. The artist was paid in beer and cigarettes, as well as occasionally nylon underwear for his female pals. It's important to note that despite nose art being a common practice, the military leadership did not formally sanction it. However, many commanders turned a blind eye to this form of expression, recognizing its positive impact on the morale of their aircrews.

Artistic crew member painting The Uninvited logo.

The crew of the 7th Bombardment Group and The Uninvited. Ed Wickemeyer on the far right top row.

Training Map
"Training took me all across this country!"

Ed left his home in Kentucky on Nov. 3, 1942. This map shows the many camps where he was sent for training until he was deployed to his base in Hawaii in May, 1944.

Ed's Travel Notes Across the USA
Where I have been and how I traveled and the time it took...

Left **Fort Thomas, Kentucky** at 9 o'clock in the morrning of Nov 3,1942 arrived at **Smyrna Air Base Smyrna Tennessee** that night at 6 o'clock. Went by way of **Louisville** and **Bowling Green Kentucky** to **Nashville**, from **Nashville** to **Smyrna** by truck.

Left **Smyrna** at 11:30 o'clock the night of Jan. 6, 1943 to **Walnut Ridge Arkansas**. Went by way of **Nashville** and **Memphis Tennessee** then went over the **Mississippi** river at 2:10 o'clock in the afternoon of Jan. 7, 1943 Arrived at **Walnut Ridge** at 6 o'clock that night.

Left **Walnut Ridge** Jan. 12, 1943 at 1:45 o'clock in the afternoon by way of **Memphis** through **Mississippi** to **Birmingham Alabama** to **Atlanta Georgia** to **Augusta Georgia** up through **South Carolina** up to **Rocky Mount North Carolina** down to **Goldsboro N.C.** to **Seymour Johnson Field** (AFB) **North Carolina**, January 14, 1943 at 9:30 o'clock at night.

Left **Goldsboro N.C.** At 3:30 o'clock in the afternoon of June 10, 1943, we went by way of **Raleigh N.C. Dunham** to **Greensboro N.C.** at 8:30 o'clock that night, I went to bed at 1:00 o'clock we got into **Asheville N.C.** at 11:00 o'clock the next morning June 11, 1943, left at 3:45 o'clock that afternoon and we arrived in **Knoxville Tennessee** at 12:00 o'clock that Midnight. We went through the Smokey Mts. We arrived at **Lexington Ky.** at 7:00 o'clock Saturday morning. June 12, 1943 left **Lexington** at 7:10 o'clock and arrived at **Cincinnati Ohio** at 10:00 o'clock in the morning. Left at 10:10 o'clock in the morning of Saturday June 12. 1943. We went through **Dayton O., Springfield O., Middletown O.,** and **Toledo Ohio** at 3:15 o'clock in the afternoon then to **Detroit Michigan** at 4:30 o'clock in the evening of Saturday, June 12, 1943.

Left **Detroit Michigan** at 8. o'clock at night on July 13, 1943 went by way of **Ypsilanti Michigan, Hicksville Ohio** and to **Baer Field Ft. Wayne Indiana** at 10:00 o'clock at night July 13, 1943. Left **Ft Wayne Ind.** 10:20 o'clock at night on July 19, 1943 got into **Huntington Ind.** At 11:00 o'clock the same night we crossed the **Mississippi** river at 7:45 o'clock in the morning July 20, 1943 and got into **St. Louis** at 8:10 o'clock that morning. Left **St. Louis** at 2: o'clock in the afternoon July 20, 1943 and arrived at **Knob Noster, Missouri** at 6:30 o'clock that same evening and went to **Sedalia Air Base** by army truck 1.5 miles away.

Left **Sedalia Air Base** at 6:00 o'clock July 26, 1943 in the evening and arrived at **Kansas City Mo.** at 7:10 o'clock that same evening. Left

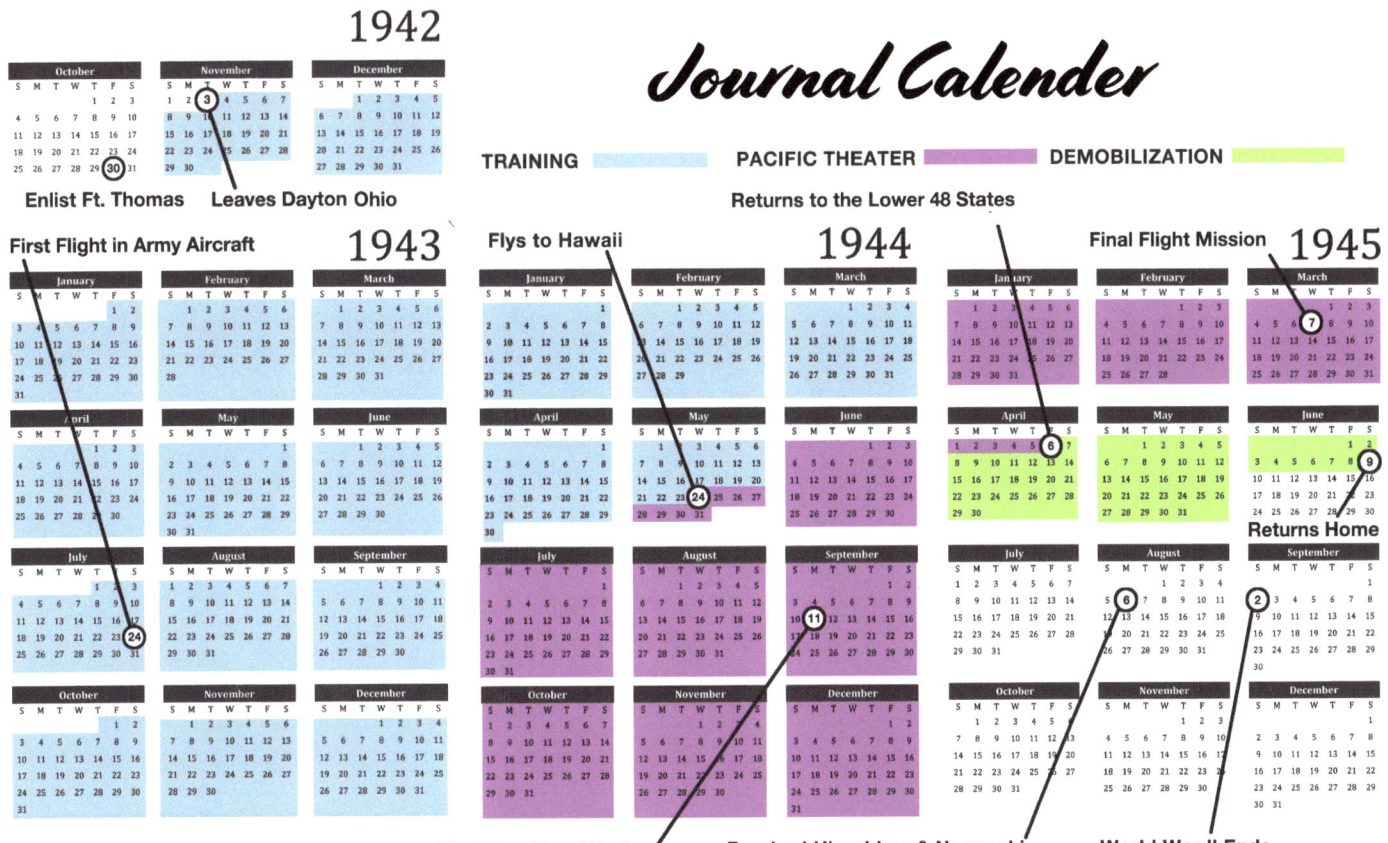

Kansas City at 10:50 o'clock that night. Arrived at **Amarillo Texas** at 3:25 o'clock in the afternoon of July 27, 1943. Went by way of **Wichita Kansas**. We left **Amarillo Texas** at 4:25 o'clock that same afternoon, arrived at **Clovis New Mexico** at 6:45 o'clock that night and left at 8:00 o'clock that night then we arrived at **Gallup New Mexico** at 7:15 o'clock in the morning of July 28, 1943. It took us 14 hours to go through the **Rocky Mts.** in **Arizona,** we got into **Kingman Arizona** at 7:45 o'clock the night of July 28, 1943. and we got into **Needles, Calif.** at 9:15 o'clock that night we left at 11:30 o'clock that night and got into **Los Angeles** at 9:45 o'clock in the morning of July 29, 1943 went to **Long Beach** by truck.

Left **Long Beach Calif.** at 1:25 o'clock in the afternoon of Sept. 1, 1943. by bus to **Los Angeles.** Left **los Angeles** at 6:20 o'clock that evening we got into **Yuma Arizona** at 3:30 o'clock in the morning of Sept. 2, 1943. We got into **Douglas** at 4:00 0clock that evening and we got into **El Paso Texas** at 10:15 o'clock that night, left at 2:05 o'clock the morning of Sept. 3, 1943. and arrived at **Kansas City Mo.** at 2:00 o'clock Sat. morning Sept. 4, 1943. Left **Kansas City** at 7:30 o'clock that morning and arrived at **Warrensburg Mo.** at 8:45 o'clock Sept. 4,1943 and went to **Sedalia Air Base** by truck.

Left **Cincinnati Ohio** at 1:00 o'clock in the morning of Oct. 8, 1943. and arrived at **St. Louis Mo.** at 9:30 o'clock that morning. Left **St. Louis** at 2:00 o'clock and arrived at the Air Base at 6:30 o'clock that evening After being home on my first fulough. **Left Sedwalia Mo.** At 2:20 o'clock in the afternoon of Oct. 28,1943. and got into **St. Louis Mo.** at 5:15 o'clock that same afternoon. Left **St. Louis** at 10:40 o'clock that night and arrived at **Little Rock Ark.** at 8:05 o'clock in the morning of Oct. 29,1943. arrived at **Texarkana Texas** at 1.30 o'clock in the afternoon that same day left **Texarkana** at 4:50 o'clock that afternoon. Arrived at **San Antonio** at 8:30 o'clock in the morning of Oct. 30,1943. stayed there all that day and night left at 10:00 o'clock in the morning of Oct. 31,1943. Arrived at **Laredo Texas** at 2.15 o'clock in the afternoon that same afternoon we went to the air base by G. I. truck.

Left **Laredo** at 3:15 o'clock in the morning of Jan. 5 1944. and arrived at **San Antone Texas** at 7:35 o'clock and left at 7:50 o'clock that same morning went through **Austin, Texarkana, Texas** and **Little Rock Ark**., arrived at **St.Louis** at 8:45 in the morning of Jan 6,1944 Left **St. Louis** at 9:00 o'clock that same morning and arrived in **Cincinnati, Ohio** at 6:50 that evening on my delay in route to **California.**

Left **Cincinnati Ohio** at 12 o'clock Saturday Morning Jan. 22,1944 Arrived in **Indianapolis Ind.** at 1:20 that afternoon and left at 1:45 and arrived at **Chicago Ill.** at 6:30 that evening and left at 9:00 o'clock that night. Arrived at **Omaha Neb.** at 8:50 o'clock in the morning of Jan. 23,1944 and left at **Omaha Neb.** at 9:35 that morning.

We arrived at **Cheyenne Wyoming** at 9:00 o'clock in the evening of Jan. 23, 1944. Left at 9:40 o'clock that same night arrived at Ogden Utah at 9:00 o'clock in the morning of Jan. 24, 1944 and left at 10:50 o'clock that same morning. Arrived **Reno Nev.** at 2:30 o'clock in the morning of Jan 25, 1944 and arrived at **Sacramento Calif.** At 9:15 o'clock in the morning of Jan 25,1944 and left at 11:00 o'clock that morning by Greyhound bus and arrived at **Fresno** at 6:00 o'clock that evening Jan. 25, 1944. Went by way of **Stockton, Merced, Madera, Calif.**

Left **Hammer Field Fresno Calif.** at 1:10 o'clock in the afternoon of Feb. 4, 1944 went through **Madera, Merced, Stockton Calif.** We got into **Stockton** at 6:15 o'clock that evening and arrived at **Sacramento** at 8:00 o'clock that night and left at 1:30 o'clock in the morning of Feb 5, 1944 arrived at **Reno Nevada** at 9:30 oclock that morning and left at 7:55 that night arrived at **Tonopah** at 2:30 o'clock in the afternoon of Feb. 6, 1944. went to air base by G.I. truck 8 mi. away.

Left **Tonapah** at 1:30 o'clock in the morning of April 28, 1944 and arrived at **Reno** at 7:30 that same morning, arrived at **Hamilton Field** at 7:30 o'clock in the morning of April 29, 1944. We went to **Fairfield Air Base** by plane left **Hamilton** at 10:30 o'clock on the morning of May 5, 1944 and landed at **Fairfield Calif.** at 11:45 that same morning. We flew from **Fairfield Calif.** to **Hawaii** on May 24, 1944.

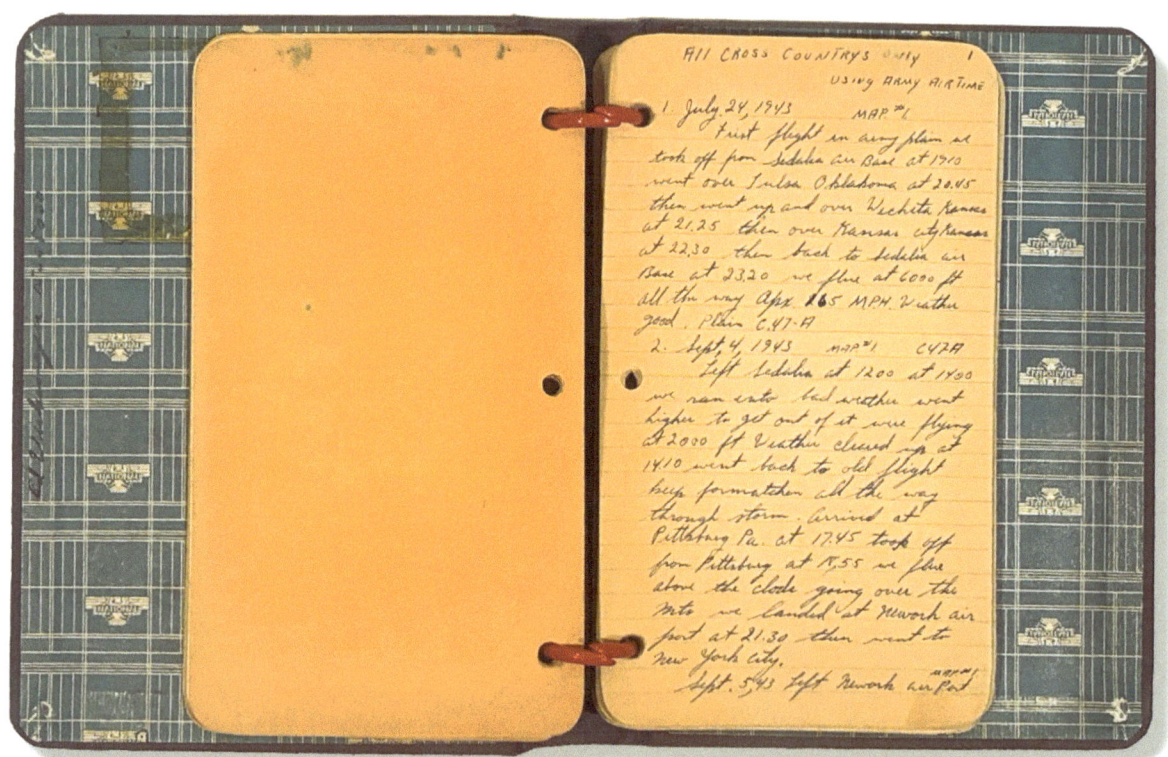

Ed's hard cover journal reprensented in regular type. (5.5" x 7.5")

Ed's pocket journal, represented in **bold type** (3.5" x 6.")

Page 8

The Journals

Ed posing in flight jacket, 1944.

Ed posing in sheepskin flight suit, 1944.

Ed posing in flight suit and gas mask, 1944.

- **First Flight:** Here you will find the first entries in Ed's Journal of actually flying in a B-24 after a tremendous amount of basic training in the continental United States.

- Very cold temperatures from high-altitude flying in unpressurized cabins required the crew to wear bulky leather and shearling jackets. Waist gunners suffered the most as they fired their guns through open window gun-ports. Ed was both wast gunner and flight engineer.

- On December 15th, 1942, Ed obtained his diploma for basic military and technical training, but that was not the end of it. Before departing on his first mission on September 11th, 1944, he had ultimately completed 21 months of training—12 on the US mainland and 3 in Hawaii followed by 6 months of air combat and bombing attacks.

All Cross Country
(Only Using Army Airtime)

1. July 24, 1943

First flight in Army plane, we took off from Sedalia Air Base at 19:10 went over Tulsa Oklahoma at 20:45 then went up and over Wichita Kansas at 22:30 then back to Sedalia Air Base at 23:20 we flew at 6000 ft all the way Apx (approximately) 165 MPH weather good. Plane C.47 - A

2. September 4, 1943

Left Sedalia at 12:00 at 1400 we ran into bad weather, went higher to get out of it, we were flying at 2000 ft. Weather cleared up at 14:10 went back to old flight keep formation all the way through storm. Arrived at Pittsburg Pa. at 17:45 took off from Pittsburg at 18:55 we flew above the clouds going over the Mts we landed at Newark Air Port at 21.30 then went to New York City. Plane C47 A

3. September 5, 1943

Left Newark Airport, weather flew 5000 ft at 190 MPH

4. September 27, 1943

Took off from Sedalia at 8:50 shuttle run to Dayton, Ohio. We landed at Stout field Ind at 11.30 and took off at 12.15 we landed at Dayton Ohio at 13:45 then I went home to start my first furlough. Weather good flew at 4000 ft all the way.

● **Tonopah Air Field** in Neveda was completed in 1941. It's Air Corps Gunnery School began on June 16th. of that year.

● **Hamilton AAF Story**
In response to the growing crisis in the Pacific, on December 6, 1941, the 30th Bombardment Group with Six B-17's left Hamilton Field in California bound for Hickam Field, Hawaii on their way to the Philippines to reinforce the American Eastern Air Force there. None of the planes were armed. They flew all through the night arriving over Oahu on the morning of December 7, 1941, and faced an unusual welcome. The B-17s had arrived over Oahu during the Japanese air attack on Hawaii which triggered the American entry into World War II. They arrived at Pearl Harbor at the height of the attack (radar operators mistakenly thought that the Japanese attack force was this flight arriving from California). Two of the planes managed to land on a short strip at Haliewa, one made a belly-landing at Bellows, one set down on the Kahuku Golf Course, and the remainder landed at Hickam under the strafing of Japanese planes.

5. March 10, 1944

Took off from Tonapah Nevada at 16:45 o'clock flying at 14,000 ft at 165 MPH Flew over Death Valley at 17:35 arrived over Los Angeles at 18:00 and then flew to Las Vegas arrived over Las Vegas at 19.07 and landed back at Tonopah at 20:00 Airplane was a B-24 - D weather good all the way.
Tonapah - L.A. 250 Miles
L.A. - Las Vegas 202 Miles L.V. -
Tonapah150 mi

6. March 27, 1944

Took off from Tonapah Nevada at 07:40 and arrived over Phoenix, Arz. At 09:30 then back up and arrived over Bolder Dam at 11:15 and landed back at Tonopah at 13:30, we flew at 16,000 ft all the way, was a little cold - 18 degree C. weather clear - in B-24

7. March 28, 1944

Went to Tucson, Arz lost track of time.

8. May 5, 1944

Flew from Hamilton Field CA. to Fairfield CA. left Hamilton at 10:30 and get into Fairfield at 11:45

9. May 13, 1944

Left Fairfield at 1:45 and went to Sacramento then to Bakersfield and back to Fairfield and landed at 19:00 we flew at 8,000 ft weather good Airplane B-24 - J

10. May 24, 1944

Left Fairfield Air Base at 0:15 and we passed over the Golden Gate Bridge at 05:40 for my last look at the U.S. for awhile and arrived at Hickem field O'ahu Hawaii at 20:00 that night, weather good flew at 7,500 ft. at 150 M.P.H. flying time 14.50 Plain B - 24 J.

Front gate to Tonapah, Nevada Airforce base. (NAC)

Sedalia Postcard 1944. (NAC)

Sedalia Army Airforce Base, NH. (NAC)

Hamilton Field, CA. (NAC)

Golden Gate Bridge, San Francisco, 1944. (USG Warchives.com)

● **Hamilton AAF**
Located in Marin county California. First established in the 1920's Originally housed bombers for the 7th Bombardmentgroup in 1934.

Softies Ice Cream Stand in the barracks at Hamilton AFB 1944. (NAC)

Hamilton Field, CA. (NAC)

Kahuku Army Airforce Base 1945. A B-24 mother ship escorting two rare Culver PQ-14 radio-controlled planes, with the runways of Kahuku AAB visible below. (NAC)

Hickam Field and Pearl Harbor looking toward Diamond Head in the distance, 1941.
(National Archives Hawaii)

● **Kahuku AAF** was a wartime airfield in Hawaii. Located on the northern tip of O'ahu, it was used for training of B-24's and B-17's pilots until March 1946. The airfield was ideal for training because it had a good approach, runway length, and take off clearance.

● **Johnston Atoll.** The total land area of this island is approximately 2.67 square miles. During World War II, it served as an important stopover and refueling station for the United States Navy and Army Air Forces. It played a crucial role in supporting the Pacific theater of the war, particularly in the Central Pacific region. Today, it is a National Wildlife Refuge managed by the U.S. Fish and Wildlife Service, with restricted access due to environmental and safety concerns.

● **Eniwetok Atoll** in the Marshall Islands is a large coral atoll of consisting of 40 islands with a total land area less than 2.26 sq miles. Since 1914 the islands had been in the control of the Japanese. The deep central lagoon is 50 miles in circumference. The Battle of Eniwetok (refered to as D-Day in the journal) was a battle of the Pacific campaign fought between February 17, 1944 and February 23, 1944. After successfully capturing Eniwetok it provided an airfield and harbor to support attacks on the surrounding Japanese controlled islands. The Uninvited B-24's first bombing mission took off from Eniwetok Airstrip on September 11, 1944.

11. August 6, 1944

Took off from Kahuku Air Field at 21:00 and flew to Johnston Island arrived over Johnston Island at 01:25 on Aug. 8, 1944 and started back to Oahu Island, arrived at Kahuku Air Field at 07:40 that morning flew at 8,000 ft weather good air speed 175 plain B-24 J.

12. August 24, 1944

Took off from Kahuku at 8:30 on flight to Palmyra, Illnois. Arrived there at 15:45 flew at 9.000 ft 160 M.P.H. #3 engine went out about 2 hrs before we got there, flew on 3 engines at 6,000 ft. Took off from Palmyra at 09:00 Aug 25, 1944 and arrived back at Kahuku at 15:45 came back with another crew. Plain B -24 .J Weather bad.

13. September 3, 1944

Left Kahuku and flew to Hickam took 45 mi. Left Hickam at 14:45 and landed at Johnston Island at 19:30 took off from Johnston Island at 07:15 on Sept 4 arrived at Kwajalein at 16:30 Sept 5, 1944.

14. September 10, 1944

Mission No. 1 Left at 15:00 Sept 10. Arrived at Eniwetok at 17:45 that day. Left Eniwetok Sept 11, 44 at 06:45 arrived over Eten Island in the Truk Atoll at 16:50 and landed there arrived back at Eniwetok at 15:15 and left at 18:30 that same night and arrived back at Kwajalein at 21.20 (9:20 PM) that night Sept. 11.

Eniwetok Island, Eniwetok Atoll, Marshall Islands. A B-24 "Liberator" bomber takes off from Eniwetok's airfield, 1944. Note: The barracks are in the distance close to the beach. (NAC)

● **Etten Island** (also spelled Eten) is located inside Chuuk Lagoon (previously known as Truk Lagoon), in the Federated States of Micronesia. It is located just to the south of Dublon Island.
This small island was bulldozed extensively by Japanese forces (who called it Takeshima during World War II) to turn it into an airstrip. There are remains of military buildings and wrecked aircraft on the island. Visitors can also climb Mount Uinku.

Dublon Island is in the center, with **Eten Island** just behind and to the right. **Moen Island** (just out of view) would be below Dudlon. 16 February 1944. (NAC)

● **Operation Hailstone** was an attack on the Imperial Japanese Navy Base located on the various **Turk Islands**, February 17-18 1944. The United States Navy conducted a massive air and surface attack on the Lagoon. This strike destroyed a large part of the Japanese military defense force including 250 warplanes, 17,000 tons of stored fuel, and about forty ships. Two light cruisers, four destroyers, nine auxiliary ships, and about two dozen cargo vessels were all sunk. After the initial attack, these Japanese bases were left to themselves without hope of resupply or reinforcements. The **Uninvited B-24** and other US military bombers would frequently drop their payloads on these islands to keep them in check. Truk Lagoon is renowned today as a tourist destination for divers interested in seeing the many shipwrecks left after the attacks by Allied forces.

The following missions are the same route and about the same time No 2. - #3 #4 #5. #7.

Mission #1 September 11, 1944 Flt A3
Target Eten Island -Truk Atoll

The weather was good we ran up against about 6 fighters. We knocked down one. The bombs hit the target hard, we used 10-500 lb GP bombs. We put the air strip out of commission for awhile and probably destroyed a radio shack. I never fired a shot, but the rest of the crew did. The fighter that was knocked down came in from the nose and broke away at about 9 o'clock. Scared, I was a little, but after the fighters came in I didn't have time for it. Flak was not very thick but there was a short burst that was out of range. Total time: 11:50, -2 landings.

Mission #2 September,15, 1944 Flt C2
From Eniwetok

Flight North Moen Island Truk. There were a lot of clouds over the target. Our ship was the only ship that dropped bombs on that part of the Island. The rest bombed South Moen. About 5 fighters hit us, not much flak. One fighter was shot down, I didn't get to shoot at him. I did shoot up about 150 rounds. 10-500 lb GP bombs were used. We could not see the bombs hits. Some phosphorus bombs were dropped at us and some frag, but no hits were made with this. Total time: 9:10.

Misson #3 September 19,1944 Flt C3
From Eniwetok
Target North Moen Island Truk

The target was hit very hard with 10- 500 lb GP Bombs. Ran into about 4 or 5 Zeros. Not much flak and about 4 phosphorus bombs were thrown at us but not too close. I got a few shots at 2 fighters. I think I got a few hits, but nothing

• **"The Whole Nine Yards."** There are many references to the origin of this phrase, some actually predate World War I. But one of the most popular urban legends is that the expression cropped up during World War II. The standard U.S. aircraft machine gun ammo belt was 27 feet long or nine yards. When a gunner exhausted his ammunition, he was said to have given his enemy "the whole nine yards."

• **Kwajalein Atoll** is in the heart of the Marshall Islands. Total land area of the atoll is just over 6 square miles. The island was taken over from the Japanese in a battle that took place from January 31st to February 3rd 1944. Kwajalein was utilized as a base for submarines, surface warships, and air staging for future military advances.

to amount to anything. They came in at 3 o'clock, I shot about 125 rounds of ammo. Weather was good. Flew at 21,500 feet. The runway on Moen had several good hits on it and I think it will be useless for about a week or so. Smoke was seen from bomb hits south of runway. All in all good bombing. Total time: 12:10, 2-landings.

Mission #4 September 25, 1944 Flt D3
From Eniwetok
Target Eten Island Truk.

We hit the target very hard. We had 10- 500 lb GP bombs but our other ships had 4- 1000 lb bombs. The flack was pretty bad. Had one small piece of flack hit our cowing on #1 engine and lodge in the mount. The flack was very close this time. Four fighters hit us and threw phosphorus bombs, one burst hit close to the right wing tip. I got a few shots at one Zero that came in from 2 o'clock and pulled up at 3 o'clock. One fighter snuck up on us about 40 miles away from the target going home but didn't come in very close. Other ships in raid hit shipping in harbor. Eton was hit with all the bombs but 6 out of all 15 Planes. Total time: 11:50, 2-landings.

Mission #5 October 2, 1944 Flt C2
From Eniwetok
Target Dublon Island Truk

We hit the Sea plane west of the Island, bombs hit wooded section east of target and the largest flack was a little ruff but most of it was low. We dropped 10- 500 lb GP bombs. 2 fighters came up to meet us each one marked one plane and threw one phosphorus bomb opener at us and left. I stood in the bomb bay, I had no gun position on this trip. I was first Engineer and Glenn fired the top turret. Mickie didn't go, he was in the Hospital. All in all mission was fair. Total time: 11:10, 2-landings.

Mission #6 October 7, 1944
From Kwajalein
Target Wake Island

We flew over the target at 10,000 feet. Had a hard time finding it for the clouds, they were very thick and low. All bombs hit land. We used 10- 500 lb GP bombs. No fighters or flak was sent up at us. I was in the top turret. One search light was turned on but went out right away. I saw a car or truck going along a road with lights on. Total time: 5:00.

15. October 7 - 8, 1944
Mission No. 6 Took off from Kwajalein at 1900 Oct 7, 1944 to bomb Wake Island. We were over the island at 24:20 and bombed it after flying over it about three times for we had a hard time finding it for the clouds. Landed back at Kwajalein at 04:20 Oct 8, 1944.

Air strip on Kwajalein Island, 1944. (NHHC)

"One Damned Island After Another"

There was a well-know saying amongst the crew members aboard a B-24 Bomber. The phrase "One damned island after another" came to represent the repetitive and challenging nature of the Pacific campaign. The Pacific Ocean is the largest and deepest Ocean on the planet. It holds the record for the most islands in the world, and there are about 25,000 islands in the Pacific Ocean. Some of the islands The Uninvited bombed or made landings on throughout their more than 40+ missions are shown on the map below.

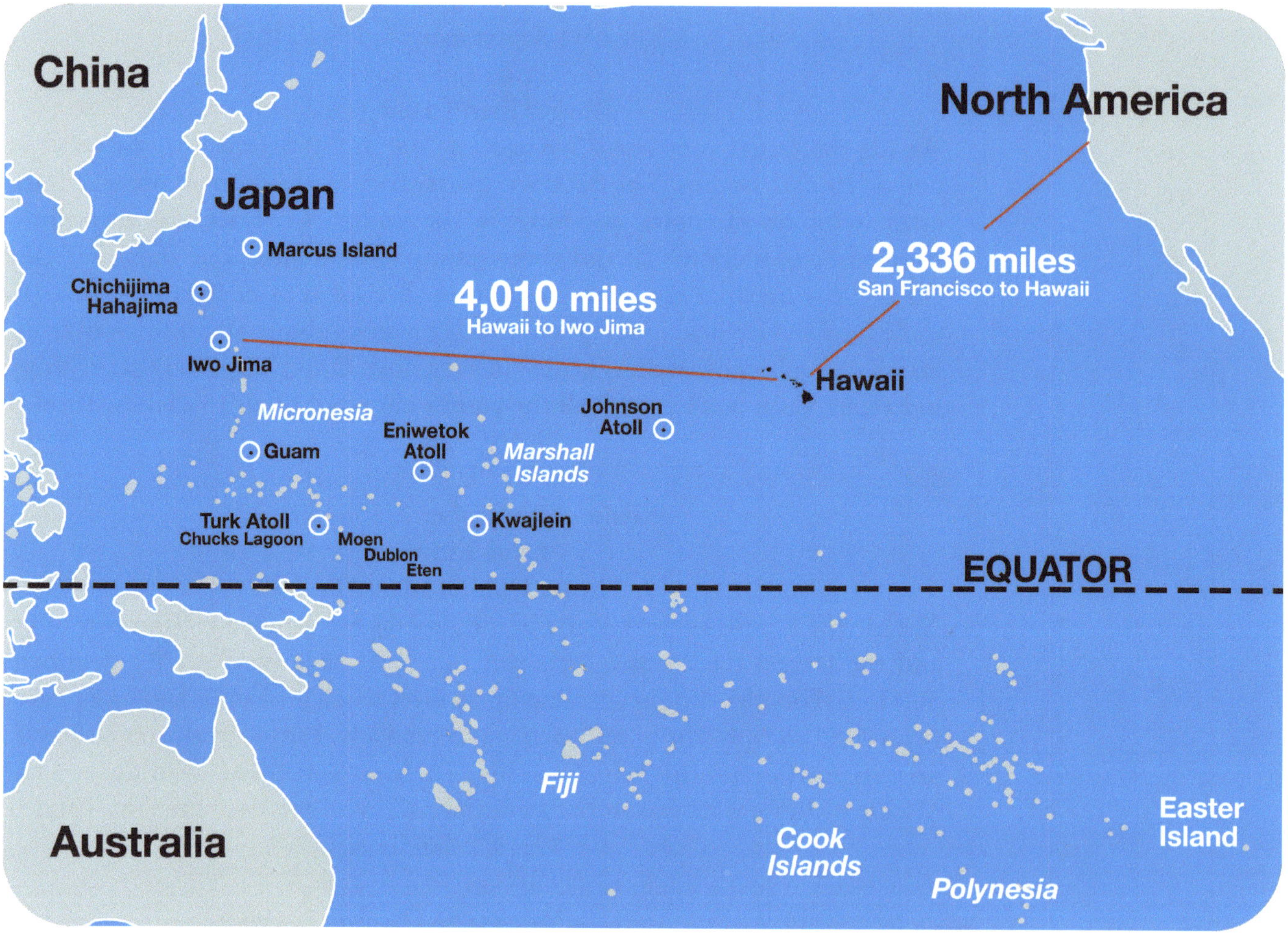

Map of the Pacific Theater of Operations

Distance from San Francisco 2,336 mi.

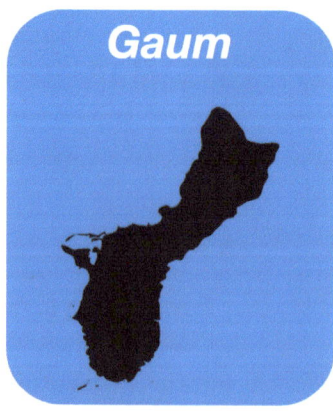

Distance from Hawaii 3,945 mi.

Distance from Hawaii 4,010 mi.

● In January 1944, the U.S. launched Operation Flintlock with the objective of neutralizing Japanese airfields and defensive installations in the Marshall Islands. The islands, including **Kwajalein, Majuro,** and **Eniwetok**, were essential to the Japanese as they provided a defensive perimeter and served as bases for their naval and air forces.

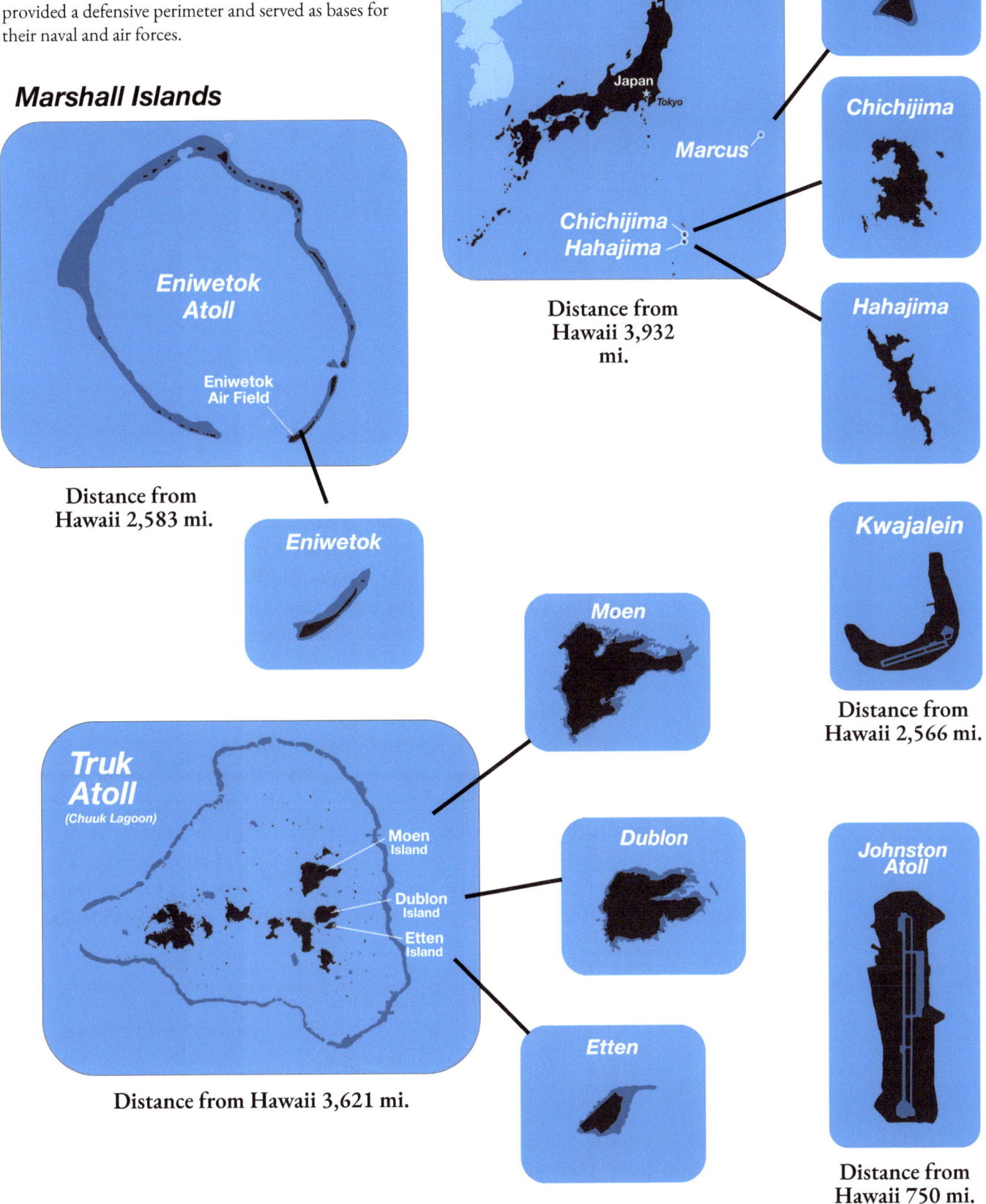

- **"The Flying Coffin"** was a nickname used by Liberators who perceived the aircraft to be unsafe and hard to fly. Its controls were stiff and heavy to maneuver and it had poor low-speed performance, especially when fully loaded with 500 lb bombs. Another drawback was it was much more vulnerable to enemy flak than its cousin the B-17.

- **Flak:** anti-aircraft fire from enemy guns and artillery. Flak as used in World War ll was a large shell that when fired, traveled to the target area and exploded within its general area, hopefully scoring a hit by filling the skies with shrapnel. Very different in modern designs, which are called "Anti-Aircraft-Artillery." Today's close-range solutions offer a bit more precision than just spamming the sky with shells and hoping to do some damage.

- **Island Hopping Campaign:** During the Pacific War, the Allies employed an "island hopping" strategy to advance towards Japan. B-24 bombers played a crucial role in supporting this campaign by targeting Japanese-held islands, airfields, and naval installations, weakening their defensive positions and providing support to ground troops.

B-24's flying over Iwo Jima. (WikiCommons)

Mission #7 October 10 Flt D2
From Eniwetok
Target North Moen Island Truk

We hit the runway. We carried 4- 1000 lb GP bombs but other ships had 10- 500 lb bombs. There were about 4 fighters came after us and threw about 6 phosphorus bombs at us. The flak was bright, it was all 75 MM and most of it was low. I fired no gun this time, I was in the bomb bay. This target was hit pretty good but not as good as other time. Total time: 10:00, 2-landings.

Mission #8 Flt D3 October17 ,1944
From Eniwetok
Target Eten Island Turk

I never got to see much of the action going around up in the air for I was in the back taking the pictures of the bomb hits. I took 3 pictures. There were 5 to 4 fighters hit the flightier we had 15 ships hit the target. We used both 4- 1,000 lb GP bombs and 10- 500 lb GP bombs. We carried 10- 500 lb bombs. The Island was covered with bomb bursts but there were a few bombs hit the water. I saw one fighter and I never fired a shot. Total time: 11:05, 2-landings.

16. Oct. 23, 1944

Took off from Kwajalein at 9:40 and we saluted the field by flying over it at 350 ft. Then we started on our way to Guam. We flew around the Island of Guam once and then we landed at 18.20 the same day. Total time 9:00.

17. Nov. 1. 44 Mission #9

Took off from Guam at 6.44 and got in formation and started off for the Volcano Islands. We were over our target Iwo Jima and bombed shipping at 12.05 and then came back and landed at Guam at 16.30 that evening. Weather fair. Alt 19000 ft. Total time 10:20.

- **Long Range Missions:** The B-24 Liberator was known for its long-range capabilities, which allowed it to conduct missions over vast stretches of the Pacific Ocean. These missions were often extremely long and could last for many hours, with aircrews enduring cramped conditions and limited facilities during the flight.

- **Enemy Resistance:** Japanese fighter planes and anti-aircraft fire posed constant threats to B-24 bombers. Dogfights and aerial battles were common during these missions, requiring skilled pilots and vigilant gunners to defend against enemy attacks.

- **Kita Iwo Jima:** is the northernmost island of the Volcano Islands group of the Bonin Islands, 50 miles north of Iwo Jima.

- K-20 USAAF Arial Camera. often used by Ed to record military events while in the air. Camera used a 9"x9" film.

K-20 Arial camera. (NAC)

Mission #9 FLT D#3 November 1, 1944
From Guam
Target Iwo Jima Volcano Islands.
We were at the target and spotted 3 ships and we went to bomb them they were right off shore from the Island. There was one plane up by us but he never came in, there was a lot of flak. The sky was full of it but it was out of range. We dropped 4- 500 lb GP bombs but no one hit any of the ships, they all hit in back of them. We then went around and came over the Island again and got lot more flak. Then we went home. Flying time 10hr 20min. I was a little scared at first, then I was OK. Total time 10:20.

Mission #10 November 5, 1944
Aborted mission.
Turned back about 1:30 hrs out. Total Time 3:00

18. Nov. 9. 44 Mission #10
Same route as 17. Took off from Guam at 09.03 on snooper mission to HaHa Jima & ChiChi Jima we flew up at 11,800 ft and about 100 miles out from the islands we went down to 200 ft. to stay out of their radar were around HaHa Jima at 13.45 and were at ChiChi Jima at 14.25 we also straffed KITA Iwo Jima a rock 30 miles south of HaHa Jima there were some Jap landing boats there after not finding any shipping around we went up to 12,000 ft and bombed HaHa Jima. Total time 12:50.

Mission #10 November 9, 1944 Flt A#2
From Guam
Snooper mission to Ha Ha Jima and Chi Chi Jima. We flew at 200 ft. and took pictures of the 2 Islands. On our way up we passed Kita-Iwo-Jima and strifed some landing boats and the shore line. We never found any shipping around the Islands so I went up to 12,000 ft. and bombed the south town on the Island of HaHa Jima, we had 4- 500 lb Gp bombs. The target was covered with clouds so we had a hard time bombing and all bombs hit in the water. There were about 50 bursts of flak, but all high. Then we all came home. I took 14 pictures with K20 Camera. Total time 12:50.

19. Nov. 13, 44 Mission # 11
About the same time as #17 but we went first to ChiChi Jima then over HaHa Jima which we covered and then to Iwo Jima which was also covered flew at 18,000 ft over all islands. They only got pictures of HaHa Jima (Navy took the pictures we escorted them for protection against fighters.) All of the falling missions are in one of the Jima's. Same rout and data as #17 but times are a little different. Took off for a mission to Iwo Jima but lost #4 engine about 20 minuites from the target and had to turn back, we went over Pagan Island and droped bombs. then went back to guam and landed. Dont know yet if we got a mission for it or not! Total time 11:10.

Ground crew loading a 500 LB GP bomb.

Ground crew loading a 500 LB GP bomb.

"Flak"- anti-aircraft gun burst.

Waist gunner in a B24.

View out a waist gunner window.

Crew doing maintenance on The Uninvited.

Raid on Truk Atoll, 17 February 1944. Airfield on Etten Island burning at left, Dublon Island in the middle background.
(NHHC: 80-G-215153)

Marcus island under attack on August 31, 1943.
(NHHC: 122205)

Japanese ships under air attack in Truk Lagoon, February 1944. Dublon Island at left, Moen Island in background. (NH: 80-G-215151)

US Military on the ground in Guam. (NHHC:80-G-239420)

Aerial view of Guam, September 5th 1944. (NHHC: S-523.02)

Eten Island Airfield, Truk, 17 February 1944. Note large number of Japanese planes on the field, and numerous bomb craters. Dublon Island is in the background, at top. (NHHC: 80-G-216891)

● **Japanese Minelayer-Okinoshima** was a large minelayer of the Imperial Japanese Navy, which was in service during the early stages of World War II. She was named after the Okinoshima Island in the Sea of Japan.

● **The Norden bombsight** device used a mechanical computer that directly measured the aircraft's changing ground speed, wind speed, direction and other effects, then quickly recalculated the bomb's impact point based on these changing flight conditions.

Mission #11 November 13 1944 Flt D#2
From Guam

Escorting the navy on a photo mission over HaHa Jima, Chi Chi Jima and Iwo Jima. We flew over all the Islands at 18,000 ft. Our ships carried 4-100 lb bombs. We got over Chi Chi Jima and we dropped our bombs there, it was very cloudy. They sent up quite a bit of flak. We got a small piece of flak in our #2 engine cowling. All the other Islands were covered so we didn't go right over them. So we had to leave. There were 3 fighters in the air but none of them got very close to us, they were always very low. Total time 11:10.

Mission #12 November 17, 1944
From Guam
Target Jap Minelayer -CW South West of Ha Ha Jima

We flew over the target at 14,000 feet. The ship threw up some flack but it was all about 4,000 ft below us. The Island threw some flack but it was all high and to the left of us. No fighters came up to meet us. Our bombs all hit behind the ship close to a little rock south of the island. Bombing was very bad, weather was good. We carried 4- 500 GP bombs. Total time 11:30.

Mission #13 November 23, 1944 Flt B#2
From Guam
Target Harbor a Chi Chi Jima

We dropped our bombs on the harbor but just after we did a cloud came over and we couldn't see the bomb hits. There were about 40 bursts of flak and about 14 phosphorus shells. There wasn't any fighters sent up after us. I never fired a shot . We dropped 4- 500 lb GP bombs. We flew at 17,500 ft. The weather was good. Total time 11:00.

Mission #14 November 27, 1944 Flt C-3
From Guam
Target Iwo Jima

We went over the target right behind the 26th. We had 9- 500 lb GP Bombs, 3 of them were 12 hr delay fuses. There was a cloud over the target but part of it was open. The south part of the Island all our bombs hit the Island. There wasn't any flack or fighters. The 26th got all the flak. They must have been cleaning their guns when we went over. Total time 10:30.

Mission #15 December 1, 1944 Flt D-4
From Guam
Target Iwo Jima

We dropped our bombs at about 2:15 o'clock. The leader of the Norden Machine was off so almost all the bombs hit the water. We went full length over the island and the flak was thick. 3 fighters same up at us and made several passes at us. I got a good shot at one that made a pass at us from 3 o'clock to 6 o'clock. I shot 100 rounds at him . He shot four burst at us but no hits. The flak was very thick and the fighter threw phorsporus bombs at us. This was the first fighter attack we have gotten over the target of Iwo Jima. We carried 9- 500 lbs bombs. 3 of them had from 2 to 12 hour delay fuses in them. Total time 09:30.

- **Interphone**- According to the B-24 Training Manual, the interphone amplifier consists of a single dual-purpose tube amplifier powerful enough to allow adequate communication between all members of the crew. There were 13 interphone station boxes throughout the airship.

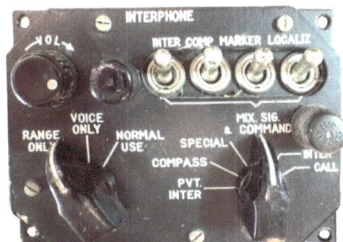

- **Radar H2X**, also known as the AN/APS-15 B-24 ground scanning radar system used for blind bombing during World War II. It was also known as the "BTO" for "bombing through the overcast" radar. It was primarily used for blind bombing missions in adverse weather conditions, such as cloud cover or darkness.

Mission #16 December 8, 1944 Flt A-3
From Guam
Target Iwo Jima

We were the second formation of B24's to go over the target. The first to hit it was 100 B-29 Superfortress with P-38 escorts and then 100 B-24's hit it. We had 9- 500 lb GP bombs. We flew at 17,500 feet. There were only 6 bursts of flak. This Island was covered with clouds and we had to find it with radar. All our bombs hit land. There was an opening in the clouds good enough for us to see the target. This raid was pre-invasion. The date of when the island was first landed on will put at bottom of this page. We saw no fighters. Total time 10:25. *Date of invasion- February 19, 1945*

Mission #17 December 11, 1944 Flt C-3
From Guam
Target Iwo Jima.

The target was open and we got very good hits on #1 Air field. We flew at 17,500 feet. The flak was pretty rough. The plane in A Flight had his engine controls on #1 & 2 engine shot out and another one had a large hole in a wing. I was taking pictures out of the hatch with Mine and Mickie's camera and did not see much flak, I saw 4 burst. There wasn't any fighters, this was another pre-invasion raid. All but 10 bombs hit the air field. We carried 9- 100 lbs GP bombs. Total time 09:50.

Mission # 18 December 15, 1944 Flt B-2
From Guam
Target Iwo Jima airfield #1 at the south end.

All of our bombs hit the target. Three fighters came in at us 5 minutes after bombs away. We shot one down, the pilot had to bail out. I shot about 75 to 100 rounds at him. The flak was rough and at our altitude and close. I had a lot of trouble with my interphone, it would cut out on me. The fighter that we shot down came in at 1 o'clock and started spinning at 5 o'clock and then went down smoking. Invasion Day is moved up, we are still going to hit Iwo Jima until invasion day. Total time 10:00.

Mission #19 December 19, 1944 Flt A-2
From Guam
Target Iwo Jima

We went over the target but couldn't see it. We bombed it with radar, we don't know whether we hit it or not. There were no fighters and no flak. We flew at 2,000 feet on the way back looking for life rafts from the B-29 crew, never saw anything. We saw one of the P.D. looking for the rafts also. We carried 9- 500 lb GP bombs. Total time 10:00.

Mission #20 December 23, 1944 Flt C-3
From Guam
Target Iwo Jima

It was very cloudy on the way up and over target and then as soon as we got

(Continued on Page 26)

The Battle of Iwo Jima

● It was determined in October 1944 that Iwo Jima had to be captured. The US Army had just introduced the B-29 "Superfortresses" into action. These huge bombers had a range capable of reaching the Japanese Home Islands. But there was a problem— Japanese fighters taking off from tiny Iwo Jima were intercepting B-29s, as well as attacking the other US airfields on nearby islands.

In 1944 **The Uninvited** dropped bombs on Iwo Jima starting on November 1st. Taking off from Guam, it ran bombing missions all through November and December 1944 and up until the U.S. Marines invaded Iwo Jima on February 19, 1945.

The Uninvited after a bomb drop on Iwo Jima, December, 1944.

Iwo Jima, February 19, 1945. (NHHC:80-G-307181)

Battle for Iwo Jima, February 19, 1945. (NHHC: 80-G-307246)

Pvt. Bob Campbell/U.S. Marine Corp/National Archives

Iwo Jima Operations, February 1945 Victors atop Mount Suribachi, Iwo Jima "Old Glory" whips against the sky as cheering Marines raise their voices and weapons in the historic moment for posterity. Note: Joe Rosenthal, photographer, is in the left foreground. Photographed by Bob Campbell, February 23, 1945. Official U.S. Marine Corps Photograph, now in the collections of the National Archives.

Flag Raising on Mount Suribachi, Iwo Jima, Japan. Local Identifier: 127-GW-319-112721; National Archives Identifier: 100310761

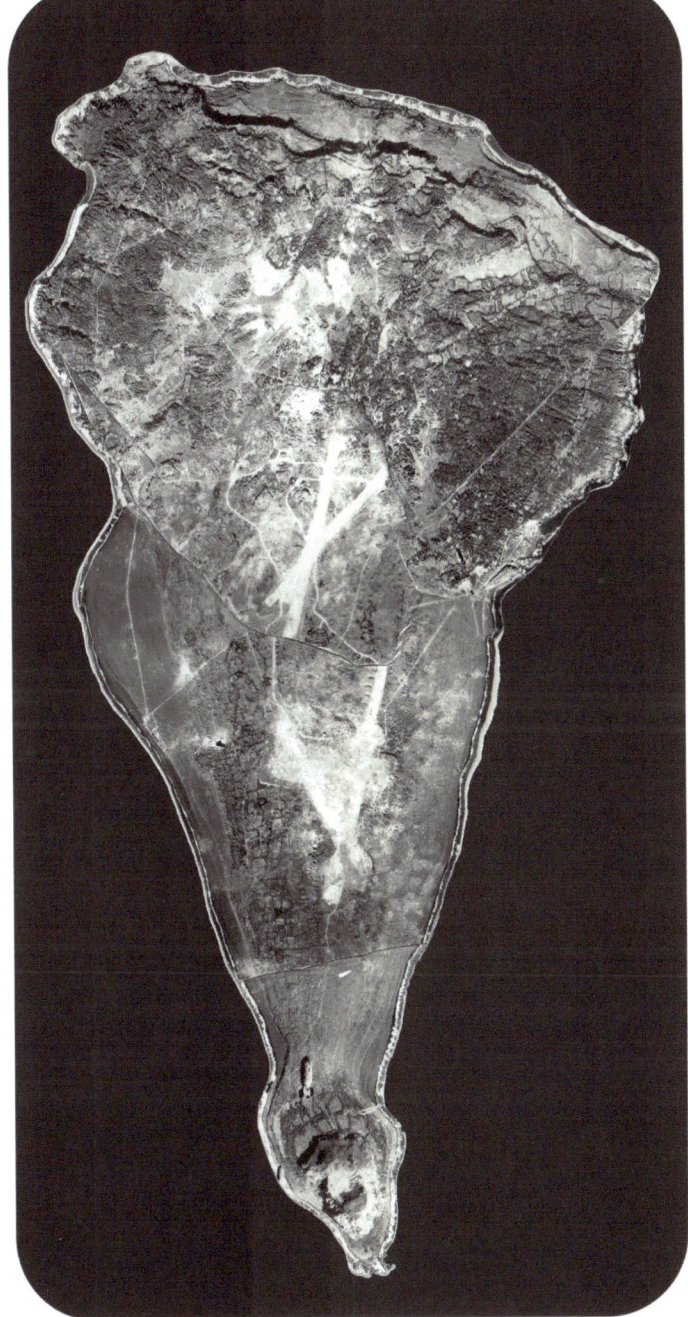

Iwo Jima, composite photo by Ed Wickemeyer

B-24 Liberators over Iwo Jima, December 12, 1944.

over the target the clouds moved away and gave us enough opening to drop our bombs on the target. All bombs but 4 hit the target. We bombed #2 airfield we had 9- 500 lb GP bombs. There were 15 bursts of flak. They were all low, they were so surprised that they didn't fire at us until after we were well past the target. There were no fighters around but there was some on the ground. We are half finished now. On the way back we went down to 800 feet and looked for life rafts again. Weather was fair on the way back. Total time 10:00.

Mission #21 December 26, 1944 Flt A-3
From Guam
Target Iwo Jima

The target was open when we got one hit, but our run was too short so we couldn't drop our bombs that time, then we tried again and wasn't able to drop them again. Then we went out for a long approach and by this time the target was starting to cover over. We dropped our bombs and they all hit land. We were hit in the bomb bay with flak and one hole in our wing. We had about 10 flack holes in us one fire hit an oxygen bottle and broke it open. We got a few flak fragments out of the shaft by the ball turret- 4 inches long and 1 inch wide. There were 2 fighters up at us 10 minutes before we dropped, they only made two passes at us, this was a rough mission. Total time 09:30.

Mission#22 December 29, 1944
From Guam

We were to bomb Iwo Jima but we lost #4 engine 20 minutes from the target and had to feather it and turn back. We dropped 6 of our 9- 500 lb bombs in the water on the way back to lighten the load and we dropped the other 3 which were delay action bombs on Fragen Island. We don't know if we got a mission for it yet or not. If we do I will write it in later. I hope that we get it. Total time 09:15. *(We got the mission) It was put in as an Iwo Jima mission.*

ABORTED Mission December 31, 1944

Turned back after blowing cylinder head from #1 engine. We were about 2 hours out. Total time 04:00. (Ed stoped recording mission length in 1945.)

Mission #23 January 6, 1945
From Guam
Target Iwo Jima

the weather over the target was bad, it was covered over with clouds and the clouds were full of ice and snow. We bombed by radar and flashes could be seen so we hit land. Some of the boys saw a little of the shoreline through the clouds. It was very cold. There wasn't any flak or fighters, we flew at 20,000 feet and had 40- 100 lb GP bombs.

Mission #24 January 10, 1945 Flt A-3
From Guam
Target Iwo Jima

We had 40- 100 lb GP bombs. We started climbing up to alt. before we got to the target and the clouds were very thick and we lost the rest of the formation. We went to 23,500 ft. before we got on top of the clouds. We flew around for a while looking for the rest of the ships then we dropped our bombs on our ETA and headed home. No flack and no fighters but it was very cold and ice started forming on the wings.

Mission #25 January 12, 1945 Flt C-2
From Guam
Target Iwo Jima

It was a little cloudy on the way up but when we got over the target it was open. We had 40- 100 lb bombs. We dropped them from 19,000 ft. There were about 35 burst of flak. The second formation from flight squadron went over the target after us and they got so much flak they had to turn around and try again. There were no fighters and 75% of the bombs hit the target.

Mission #26 January 16, 1945 D-2
From Guam
Target Iwo Jima

The target was clouded in when we got there so we had to bomb by radar. After we dropped our bombs I saw part of the coastline and saw 2 bomb flashes. We had 40- 120 lb cluster fragment bombs 6- 20 lb frags in one cluster. We bombed from 19,300 feet. There wasn't any flak or fighters, it was a little cold though.

19-b. No Date

Took off for a mission to Iwo Jima but lost #4 engine about 20 mi from the target and had to turn back. We went over Pagan and dropped bombs, then went back to Guam and landed. Don't know yet if we got a mission for it or not.

20. Jan 19, 1945

We were escorting the Navy VD5 to Iwo, HaHa, and Chi Chi Jima and we got lost and we were 400 miles from Tokyo. Then we turned around and went back to the base.

Mission #27 January 19, 1945 Flt A-2
From Guam

Escort Navy VD5 photo ships to Iwo, Ha Ha, and Chi Chi Jima. The Navy got lost but we kept on going for about 3 and 1/2 hours after we were at alt. then we turned back. We found out later that we were about 400 miles south of Tokyo and 50 miles south of the islands just below Japan proper. We had 4 - 100 lb GP bombs that we didn't drop then we brought them back. We were at 22,600 ft., no fighters no flak. It was plenty cold 20 degrees below zero.

Mission #28 January 19,1945
From Guam
Target Iwo Jima

We got up to alt. and the Island was all covered over. We dropped our bombs by radar. There wasn't any flak and no fighters We bombed from 19,000 feet. It wasn't too cold on this mission . We carried 40- 100 lb GP bombs.

Mission #29 January 22 1945 Flt A-2
From Guam
Target Iwo Jima

When we got there the clouds were just clearing from over the target and when we got on the bomb run it was fully open. All of our bombs hit the #2 air field, there were about 2 bursts of flak, it was a little close most of it was light. There was one fighter in the air, it had just taken off as our bombs hit. He never did come up to fight us. We carried 40- 100 lb GP bombs. Weather was fair but cloudy. The next day we went on rest leave and got back February 7th, 1945.

21. January 23, 1945

We took off from Guam on a C-54 at 11:15 and landed at Kwajalein at 22:05, then took off at 23:05 January 23 and landed at Johnson Island at 09:45 Jan 23rd. Passed the Date Line between Kwajalein and Johnson. Took off from Johnson at 11:40 and landed at Hawaii at 15:30. We were on our rest leave. We were there about 11 days. Took off from Oahu at 19:15 on Feb 5 and landed at Johnson at 20:40, took off at Johnson Feb 5 at 23:40 and landed at Kwajahin at 6:37 Feb. 7, 1945 took off from Kwajahin at 7:30 and landed at Guam at 13:30 - All times are local total flying time 41:30 time was not loged. Weather good.

Mission #30 February 10, 1945 Flt A-3
From Guam
Target Iwo Jima

The target was open and all of our bombs were on land, all but for the ones that bursted in the air at 1,600 feet below us. We picked up 10 P-38 escorts at Saipan. They got one Zero out from 9 o'clock high from our flight. It went up in flames. They said that they got 2 others under the clouds. We got about 300 burst of flak, it was a little close above and below and out on both sides of us. It was sure good to see those P-38's with us. We had a new type of radio fuse on our bombs and they were suppose to go off 20 feet off the ground, but they went off all over the place. The weather was good. I got 8 pictures- 5 weather-3 of targets.

Mission #31 February 12, 1945 Flt C-1
From Guam
Target Iwo Jima

The weather was clear until we got to the target and the target was covered over. We bombed by radar and one plane went down under the other. Can't see the bombs hit. He said all bombs hit the target and a fire was started. We carried 40- 100 lb GP bombs. There were no fighters and no flak. I took 6 weather pictures but could not get any bomb hit pictures because of the clouds. D-DAY HAS STILL BEEN PUT OFF.

Mission #32 February 16, 1945 Flt A-3
From Guam
Target Iwo Jima

We were to bomb at 7,500 feet if the target was open and 3,000 feet if the target was closed in but the target was so closed in we would have had to go too low to

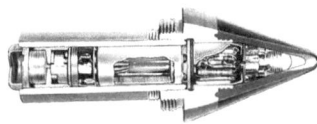

- **Radio Fuse Bombs:** these were the secret weapon of World War II. Radio Fuse air busting bombs or VT Proximity Fuses were a highly classified invention of World War II, which enabled bombs and projectiles to detonate at a set distance from the target.

- **D-Day Note:** The term D-Day is a coded designation used for the day of any important invasion or military operation. Ed's reference to D-Day was for the invasion of **Eniwetok**.

- **Lack of Proper Navigational Aids:** Unlike modern navigation systems, B-24s during World War II relied on rudimentary instruments and celestial navigation methods. Navigators used stars and landmarks to determine their position, which could be challenging during adverse weather conditions or when flying over featureless ocean expanses.

- **Crew Fatigue:** Flying long-range missions over extended periods placed immense physical and mental strain on the aircrews. The lack of pressurized cabins and comfortable seating meant that the crew endured fatigue, discomfort, and the constant risk of exposure to extreme cold at high altitudes.

bomb so we didn't, we just circled for a while. The Navy was shelling the ___?___ down. I saw one battleship firing at it. D-DAY ISN'T FAR OFF NOW. We saw 187 ships on the way to the island for the invasion, not counting the ships already there. We got no fighters and no flak, we brought our bombs back with us, we had radio fuses.

Mission #33 February 18, 1945 FLT A-2
From Guam
Target Iwo Jima

Pre-invasion bombing but the target was so covered over we could not go in to bomb. We could have come in and bombed at 2,000 ft. but we had radio fuse air bursting bombs so we couldn't go any lower than 3,500 feet. So we went home without bombing. No fighters not flak.

D-DAY (IWO JIMA) WAS FEBRUARY 19, 1945

22. Feb, 22, 1945
Took off from Guam at 0700 in the morning on our way to Marcus, we were over the target at around 1400 and dropped our bombs then came back landed at Guam at 19.20. Mission #34.

Mission #34 February 22, 1945 A-3
From Guam
Target Marcus Island

We were at 10,000 ft. but our ship's radar was out so we had to go under the clouds. We found the target after looking for it for about an hour. We went over the target at 5,500 ft. We dropped all 20- 100 lb GP bombs on the runway, there was a lot of flak and a lot of small arms that were trailing all under us. The other ships got hit, we never did. There were no fighters but flak was accurate and saturated. We found out later that there was a flak hole in our ship in the right wing.

Mission #35 February 25, 26, 1945
From Guam
Target Chi Chi Jima

It was a night mission, we had a hard time finding the island. We had to drop down to 6,000 ft. We found it and 15 g or 20 bombs hit land starting west of the airfield and giving over to the shore. We had 20- 100 lb bombs. There were no fighters and no flak and they never turned on any search lights.

Mission #36 February 27, 1945
From Guam
Target Iwo Jima Northeast

The Marines had a little over half the island. Our target showed on Northeast end. We went over the target twice, the first time C flt dropped their bombs, they hit the target area, then the rest of us dropped ours the second run. Our bombs hit the target area, all but one plane's, it went into the water off shore. There was no flak and no fighters. There was alot of attacks by the Navy the planes were dive bombing and striking. We had 9-500 lb GP bombs.

23. February 25 - 26, 1945

Took off from Guam at 15.30 o'clock on the evening Feb 25 and went up and bombed airfield at ChiChi Jima then went back and landed at Guam. Feb 26, 45 at 0420 o'clock Mission #35. - Mission 36 - same as #17 all but time difference and a target was the north end of the island. - Mission #37 - same as #23. Same target but just small time difference.

Mission #37 February 28-March 1, 1945
From Guam
Target Chi Chi Jima

We turned into the target and the bombard couldn't see the island so we made a radar run, but the pilot put it into a dive and the bombs fell just short of the island. There were no lights, no flak, no fighters on the way back. Between Chi Chi and Iwo the radar man saw a plane right behind us kept going, he came across our tail but later he came close and we saw that it was a navy F4U. We thought it was a Jap Meg Fighter at first, I was in the nose part on this flight.

Mission #38 March 2-3 1945
From Guam
Target Chi Chi Jima- Night

We made a radar bomb and just after bombs away they put 8 search lights on us and we got 21 burst of flak. It was at our altitude but wasn't too close. Our bombs all hit the target, we had one delay bomb, the rest were not. We bombed at 10,500 ft. No fighters came up to us.

Mission #39 March 4 1945
From Guam
Target Chi Chi Jima

The target was covered so we had to go down to 200 feet and watched the bombs hits and take pictures. I never saw any bombs hit but one of the boys did. I took 5 weather shots. We dropped our bombs in the water. We were going to bomb Chi Chi Jima if it was covered, but it was open and we were so low we didn't. There was no flak and no fighters.

Mission #40 March 6-7, 1945
From Guam
Target Chi Chi Jima- Night

The target was covered over and we radar bombed. Our bombs hit land for we saw the burst. We got about 17 burst of flack but it was all out of range. Three search lights were put on but they couldn't go through the clouds. No fighters. **<u>WE ARE FINISHED NOW.</u>**

24. March 28 1945

Took off from Guam at 05:45 in the morning and landed at Kwajalein at 16:55 that day and took off at 18.00 and landed at Johnson Island at 03.55 on the morning of March 28, 1945 we crossed the date line between Kwajalein and Johnson that is why the same date you gain a day when you cross the date line going east. Took off from Johnson at 05.50 we had trouble with #1 Eng. (engine) and was held up a little at Johnson we landed at Hickam at 11.25 March 28, 1945. Took off from Hickam Field Oahu Hawaii at 1600 April 5, 1945. My first view of San Francisco was the lights through the clouds. We landed at Hamilton Field at 05:35 April 6, 1945 time flying 11 hrs 35 min.

C54 - ATC. Time from Guam to Hickam 22 hrs. 15 min

ATC - C - 54

Arrived San Francisco April 6, 1945 05:30. Left San Francisco at 7:30 by plane and got to Oakland at 7:50 then got on train. The rest of the trip is by train. We left Oakland at 8:45 that night April 9, 1945

April 10, 1945 we went through Reno in the morning and arrived at Odgen Utah at 8:45 that night and left at 10:10 that same night. Got into Salt Lake City at 11:30 and left at 12:15 on the morning of April 11, 1945. We went through Royal Gorge and under Hanging Bridge Colorado. We were very low and the bridge was very pretty to look at. We got into Denver at 10:30 o'clock that night April 11, 1945 and left at 1:20 in the afternoon of April 12, 1945. Went through McCook Nebraska. at 5:30 and heard the news of President Roosevelt's death then. Went through Lincoln Neb. at 12:30 o'clock in the morning of April 13, 1945 and arrived in Chicago at 12:45 that morning April 13, 1945 and left Chicago at 11:25 that night, arrived at Edenburg Ind. at 5:45 in the morning of April 14, 1945 and went to Camp Adambury by GI Bus. Left Adambury at 4:00 that night and got in Indianapolis Ind. at 5:30 and left at 6:00 that night and arrived at Cincinnati at 9:45 on the night of April 14, 1945.

Left Cincinnati at 8:55 arrived in Chicago at 3:40 o'clock May 7, 1945 left at 8.00 that night. Arrived at Kansas City at 8:45 in the morning of May 8, 1945 and left at 9:00 that same morning arrived at El Paso Texas at 8:50 in the morning of May 9, 1945 and left at 9:20 same morning. We got out of New Mexico about 3:00 o'clock and got into Douglas Ariz. at 4:15 o'clock that afternoon we left at 4:30 went through Phoenix, Ariz. at 11:30 at night and got out of Ariz. at about 4:30 o'clock in the morning of May 20, 1945. We arrived in Los Angeles at 10:45 that morning and left at 11:45 and arrived at Santa Ana at 1:20 May 10, 1945.

Left Santa Ana at 3:25 in the afternoon June 1, 1945 and arrived in LA at 4:25, left LA 6:35 that evening went through Flagstaff Arz. at 2:10 in the afternoon of June 2, 1945, got into Gallup New Mexico at 6:15 stay about 5 min. went through albuquerque N.M. at 9:50 stayed there 15 min. went through ___?___ at 10:25 in the morning of June 3, 1945, got into Dodge City at 1:38, we were there about half an hour. Left New ton Kan. at 6:50 in the evening were there 55 mi. got into Kanasas City at 11:30 that night and left at 9:35 that morning June4, 1945. Arrived at Indianapolis at 1:50 that afternoon and left at 2:40, arrived at Edinburgh, In. at 3:30 that afternoon we went to Camp Atterbury by Grayhound Bus. Left Atterburyat 11:00 in the morning of June 9 1945, and got to Indianapolis at 2:35 June 9,1945 and arrived in Cincinnati at 6:20 that evening to go home for good.

Ed Wickemeyer Wartime Portraits

On leave in Oahu.

Lanikai Beach, Oahu.

Pineapple field in Oahu.

Tall grass in Oahu.

Kneeling in front of the Ohio River.

At base camp.

R&R in Oahu.

R&R in Oahu.

Crew members on Guam

GUAM 1944

Goldi

Our tent

Micky

Mick and 500 lb. bomb

Ed

Mel Alred

Goldie

Ed

P. Helms

Hawaii During War Time

A man can get killed that way
Brief Magazine Article, January 30th, 1945

SOUVENIR SEASON CLOSED

There will be no more souvenir hunting for the members of a 7th AAF heavy bombardment group in the Marianas. Because too many souvenir hunters were running into too many Japs and getting only a small return in keepsakes, the group's CO has declared the season closed. His reason: men trained for aerial combat were not at their best in jungle warfare.

S.Sgt. Edward W. Wickemeyer of Dayton, Ky., aerial gunner of the 7th AAF Liberator The Uninvited, agrees with his CO but, before the lid was clamped on, he did his best to prove airmen can also handle theselves on the ground.

As a veteran of 15 combat missions, Wickemeyer had more than once fired on attacking Jap planes—but always with the realization that if he shot one down there was no souvenir jackpot. In the Marianas, he saw a chance to pick up a few mementos left by the Japs and, with three other crew members, set out one day thru the thick underbrush. The group had armed themselves with carbines and automatics.

Less than a mile from their camp, the men heard voices and the sound of hammering in the brush. At the edge of a clearing they paused, and then stopped dead when they found themselves within 20 feet of a squad of Japs who were building a hut. On the opposite side of the clearing stood a sentry armed with a rifle. A Japanese officer with two pistols in his belt lay sound asleep in the shade of a tree. The men at work seemed to be unarmed.

Wickemeyer and his friends decided to go back for help. They skirted the clearing and headed for a spot where they had earlier noticed some aviation engineers at work.

Then Wickemeyer stepped on a dead branch and the jungle exploded.

The four airmen hugged the ground as Jap bullets whined over their heads and tore thru the underbrush. The Americans opened up with their carbines and when a volley spattered around the hut, the Japs broke and ran. Two Japs who had been working on the roof of the half-built shack dropped down inside. The others sought cover in the building and outside close to its frame walls, using boxes and boards but they could not get completely out of sight. Wickemeyer picked off the Jap officer and two others were shot as they returned the airmen's fire. The remaining Japs, completely outfought, finally scattered and fled for the safety of the jungle. Four more were brought down as they ran and only three of the original Japs working on the shack managed to escape.

After a cautious check-up to be sure there were no more Japs around, Wickemeyer and his friends crawled out of the bushes and looked over their catch. It was a good haul. From the officer, Wickemeyer got a Samurai sword, a valuable souvenir in any sniper-hunter's league. He came away also with a Jap-made German Luger, a Spanish .32 caliber automatic and a wristwatch. The other Japs yielded a bayonet, diary, dictionary and more than 3000 yen.

Back in his tent, Wickemeyer proudly displayed his souvenirs to other 7th AAF men. But he discouraged them from planning similar expeditions. Agreeing with his CO, Wickemeyer exclaimed, "A man can get killed that way!"

BRIEF, VOLUME 2, NO. 9 JANUARY 1945
BRIEF WAS AN AAF PUBLICATION IN THE PACIFIC OCEAN AREA.

Ed's Version
Of the Adventure

Jap Hunting -About the 2nd week of Nov. 44 Goldie and I and 2 ground crewmen went out into the woods, out past the point out the north shore of the island. We found some bear foot prints and started following them. We went up a Cliff about 1/2 way and heard some choking and went around a curve and stopped.

No more than 20 feet away were some Japs building a hut. We counted about 8 of them and heard them talking to some others so we figured about 12 to 14 of them. One of them was an officer. We looked the place over for a few minutes and decided that there were too many of them for us to handle. Some of them had guns and we only had 3 carbines and 2 - 45's so we went back to get a few more men. This time we had grenades and tomy guns. We took the wrong path and wound up underneath them and the Jap officer started shooting at us. We shot back and threw a grenade in and got him and winged another. One of the other boys got him, then one started running up the Cliff and I took 3 shots at him and so did Goldie. We wounded him and one of the boys on the other side got him. All together we killed 4 and wounded one but the next day some of the boys found him dead.

US Army soldiers 1944 (DOD)

I got an English made watch from the officer's coat and a bayonet, helmet and part of a Jap Dictionary.

Japanese soldiers, 1944 NHHC

US Army soldiers NHHC

US Army soldiers exploring the jungle NHHC

Page 37

Service Manuals

● There are a total of seven service manuals and additional training manuals for the B-24D Consolidated Aircraft. They were prepared by the Flight and Service Department of Consolidated Aircraft Corporation at Lindbergh Field in San Diego, California, October 1942.

To ease the boredom of having to drudge through these manuals, the government hired a military cartoonest named R.F. Duggan to illustrate what NOT to do while flying the aircraft. Some of these graphics are displayed here.

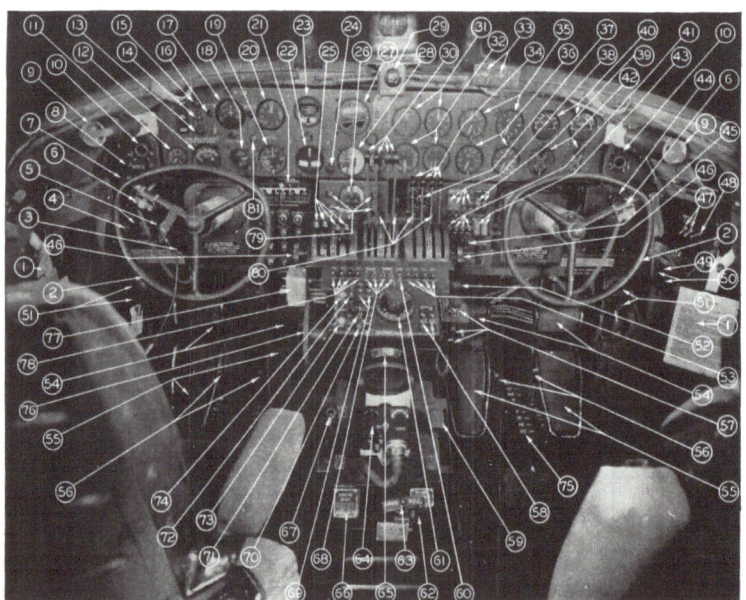

Cockpit diagram

B-24 Liberator flight manual.

R.F. Duggan Illustrations

LESTER B. BONER

Lester Boner is one of those guys
   Who tries to impress you as being wise.
As a technician he's not so bright;
   He makes no effort to see if he's right.
On critical jobs he's so likely to fail,
   We can trust him only with mop and pail.

Training Manual

Ed Wickemeyer training at gunnery camp in Laredo, Texas 1943.

PILOT TRAINING MANUAL FOR THE LIBERATOR

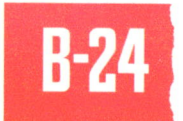

RESTRICTED

THE GUNNERS

The B-24 is a most effective gun platform, but its effectiveness can be either amplified or defeated by the way the gunners in your crew perform their duties in action.

Your gunners belong to one of two distinct categories: turret gunners and flexible gunners.

The power turret gunners require many mental and physical qualities similar to what we know as inherent flying ability, since the operation of the power turret and gunsight are much like airplane operation.

While the flexible gunner does not require the same delicate touch as the turret gunner, he must have a fine sense of timing and be familiar with the rudiments of exterior ballistics.

All gunners should be familiar with the coverage area of all gun positions, and be prepared to bring the proper gun to bear as the condition may warrant.

They should be experts in aircraft identification.

Where the Sperry turret is used, failure to set the target dimension dial properly on the K-type sight will result in miscalculation of range.

They must be familiar thoroughly with the Browning aircraft machine gun. They should know how to maintain the guns, how to clear jams and stoppages, and how to harmonize the sights with the guns.

While participating in training flights, the gunners should be operating their turrets constantly, tracking with the flexible guns even when actual firing is not practical. Other airplanes flying in the vicinity offer excellent tracking targets. Automobiles, houses, and other ground objects afford excellent tracking targets during low-altitude flights.

The importance of teamwork cannot be overemphasized. One poorly trained gunner, or one man not on the alert, can be the weak link that destroys the entire crew.

Keep the interest of your gunners alive at all times. Any form of competition among the gunners themselves will stimulate interest to a high degree.

Finally, each gunner should fire the guns at each station to familiarize himself with the other man's position and to insure knowledge of operation in the event of an emergency.

Edward William Wickemeyer
Post War Portraits

Edward Wickemeyer posing on the balcony of his home in New Palestine, Ohio, 1978. Photo taken with a handmade pinhole camera by his son Daniel Wickemeyer.

Edward Wickemeyer posing on the balcony of his hotel room while vacationing in Santa Barbara, California, March 1994. Ed passed away four months later in July, 1994.

I don't know if it's true but Ed told me...

This is a collection of remembered thoughts that Edward W. Wickemeyer shared over his lifetime with his family members. He never bragged or spoke of the war unless he was asked directly. He would then happily share his memories with us. The war had not ended when Ed returned home to Cincinnati. He quickly married Nancy McNamara and they took their honeymoon in Gatlinburg, Tennessee. Ed and Nancy had 4 children: three boys and one girl named Wes, Jennifer, Wayne, and Daniel Wickemeyer. Wes passed away in 1995. Jennifer had 3 boys of her own, Mark Jr, Michael and Matt Glassmeyer. Wayne Wickemeyer married Brenda Moore and produced Eric, Elizabeth and Nathan Wickemeyer. And Daniel married Kelly Oram and had a girl, Charlee Wickemeyer.

Mark Jr. Glassmeyer Grandson.

One Lucky Jap in camp. I think this all happened on Guam. Grandpa told me this story and I remember asking him to tell it again several times in the company of others.

Story goes that on Guam there were still Japs in the jungle that had not been captured yet. These soldiers were cut off from the other Japs and as a result many got very hungry in the jungle. So hungry in fact that some would be willing to try to sneak into the US base on the island to steal food.

On the base the tents were lined up in rows and the mess hall was more to the middle of camp. One night a Jap snuck in and was noticed by US troops. The Jap ran for his life down the middle of the tents and no one could shoot him since if they missed the shot would have gone into the tent across from the person shooting and potentially kill one of our boys. That was all but one tent Grandpa's, whose tent was at the end of the line. No tents opposite his to worry about. As the Jap approached, he grabbed his Colt 45 1911 handgun and took aim at the enemy, slowly pulled the trigger only to hear a CLICK......he did not have the gun loaded he found out .....and one lucky Jap ran off into the thick jungle with a sandwich.

Best Pranks Ever. Grandpa told me they used to save up their empty glass coke bottles until they had a good supply. When the guys were happy with the quantity of their empty coke bottle inventory they would take a string and tie two coke bottles together by the tops. On the way back from successful bombing missions flying over friendly or already captured islands, or really any island or ship, they would drop the bottle out of the bomb bay. Since they were tied together as they fell they would spin and whistle......so they sounded like bombs being dropped! The poor guys on the ground or on the ships would for a few minutes think they were being bombed.

The Distinguished Flying Cross. The story I heard was that on a bombing mission, a hidden Japanese radio shack was discovered and in response the Uninvited peeled off the formation to go down and take it out. This action of bravery was the reason for the entire crew being awarded the Distinguished Flying Cross.

~ Related story to this story years later would be when I got to go with Grandpa to their 7th Air Force 11th bomb group reunion in Oshkosh, Wisconsin. The reunion was held at the annual AirVenture Air Show. At the time every member of the Uninvited was still alive and they were all so happy to see each other, tell war stories, and catch up on the lives and families of each other. On the second night at dinner was the first time I heard the distinguished flying cross story. Just a kid when I heard the story for the first time, I thought that they had blown up a Radio Shack ...as in the retail electronics store Radio Shack. I asked why they would do that? What about all the people shopping? Needless to say the crew got a good laugh over the question and went on to explain that it was a very much different radio shack that they had taken out to help protect their buddies.

<u>**Training Trick.**</u> During training the gunners would mess with new guys by taking the 50 caliber shells that were used in all the main B-24 Model J guns and open them up. They took the projectile off the case and then took about half the gunpowder out. They then took these shells and put them back in the ammo boxes of the new guys. In training when they fired their 50 cal's the new guys would be blasting away and then 5 or so bullets would just PLOP out the end of the gun......big laugh every time I was told .

Why I did what I did...

Why I did what I did. I remember exactly where we were, on the outer loop around Chicago on our way home from Oshkosh in Grandma's new Jeep Cherokee, just Grandpa and I. We had just had a wonderful time together at AirVenture where I met every member of the Uninvited crew for the first time. Looking back now I reealise that I must have been on a "pro military" and "serving your country" high after meeting his crew for the first time and watching the display of military jets perform at the Air Show. I wanted Grandpa to know that I wanted to be as brave as he was when I grew up.

I said, "Someday Grandpa I want to fly for the Airforce and go to war to protect our freedoms like you did"
There was a long pause and even as a kid I could notice a mood change. Then Grandpa joking fun tone was replaced with a distinct serious tone.

He said, "Mark I went to war and did what I had to do so that you would NEVER have to go to war, I hope that's true and you never have to."

Mark Glassmeyer Jr. in the hotel parking lot the day Grandpa Wickemeyer took him to the Oshkosh, Wisconsin reunion.

Daniel M. Wickemeyer Son.

The Golden Gate Bridge. When they were stationed in Hamilton Field in San Francisco, Dad's crew would often do short flight runs in their new B-24J bombers. Dad once told me that their pilot Phil Swartzman, who had a rough personality, one day decided to fly under the Golden Gate Bridge. At high tide it has a clearance of 220 feet or about 73.3 yards. He made the successful pass and flew back to the base. About an hour or so later there was an announcement made over the PA reprimanding the flight and instructing everyone not do the same or they will face serious consequences. Phil became quite a hero after that.

Fourth of July Boating Trip. WEBN would celebrate the 4th of July in Cincinnati each year with a fantastic display of fireworks on the Ohio River. We owned a 40. foot houseboat, I was a high school student and my brother Wayne and I had a group of friends that were eager to go. Dad volunteered to captain the ship down the river to the Cincinnati Riverfront where the fireworks would be displayed. My Mom opted out because she thought it was a "dangerously crowded event." Dad knew that us kids really wanted to go and did not want us going at it alone. We cruised down the river, Dad had all his Coast Guard credentials that he so proudly displayed on the boat. We found a spot under a bridge with an easy exit path planned for when the show was over. I went up to the top deck to watch the show, turned on the radio to hear the sychronized music with the fireworks. Wes my oldest brother was broadcasting the sound for the show at WEBN so he could not go. At the end of the show I climbed down from the top deck and saw my Father sitting in the dark on one of the 4 bunk beds in the stern of the boat. He was holding his chest so I thought something was very wrong. I asked him are you all right? He replied, "I'm ok it's just that the arial blast at the end of the fireworks show sounded exactly like the Flak burst during the war. Just give me a minute and I'll be OK". That was the only time I ever witnessed him display any kind of PTSD. He normally held all those feelings inside and would only discuss the good memories he had with his crew to his family.

Westlund Owen Wickemeyer, first son. A bunch of friendly crew members were sitting around in the mess hall relaxing and trading mission stories with one another, when an anxious Sergeant quickly busted through the mess hall door and said "We need a volenteer bombardier to replace a sick comrade for a short mission." A friend of my father's named Sergeant Westlund proudly raised his hand and said, "I'll do it." Later that afternoon they heard a loud crashing noise and ran outside to discover that one of their B-24's on its take-off had not cleared the mountain at the end of the runway. The planes were loaded up with so many heavy bombs and lots of fuel that it made it very difficult for the pilots to safely take off. Weslund was on that flight, he did not survive. Dad promised himself he would name his first born child after that friend he lost.

Jennifer Glassmeyer, Daughter.

Ed's First Paycheck.
One spring day in May when I was about 14 years old, I was helping my father mix concrete in an old wheel barrel . He was building brick steps that led from our driveway to our back yard. My job was to hold the hose and add water to the cement mixture as he used a hoe to stir the mix. Unexpectedly, he began talking about the value of hard work and how grateful he was for all that he had. He told me of his parent's struggles to make ends meet while raising him and his younger brother. His father was a printer and his mother was a homemaker. Dad did not open up to me often about his family, so I pressed him in the moment for more information. He got quiet for a bit and then said, " My mother was a wonderful cook and she always dreamed of having a new electric stove. When I got my first month's pay check from the Air Corp, I sent it home to her with a picture I had cut out of a magazine of a new stove." He was so proud to be able to do that for her.

Love Letters to Nancy.
When my father left for basic training he had been dating my mother, Nancy P. McNamara, for only a few weeks and they already knew they wanted to keep their relationship moving forward. They promised to write each other while separated by war. Since letters from the enlisted were censored by ranking officers so that valuable information, such as group movements, would not fall into enemy hands, my father devised a plan. He would send his letters to her, addressed to her full name, but he would change her middle initial on every envelope. The middle letter would soon spell out his location. She would have to put the letters in chronological order according to the dates they were written. When her name was address without a middle initial, that was the end of that specific word. Mom laughed when she remembered sitting on the floor with her best friend arragning the envelopes, trying to figure out where Ed was.

Tora Tora Tora!
On a summer day in the late 1970's my family and I traveled 30 miles north of our home in Cincinnati to Dayton Ohio, where we were going to attend the Wright Patterson Airbase Air Show. My father was excited to show us some of the planes he flew in during the war and to see the most modern F-16's and F-18's and more! After a lovely day we gathered by the airfield fence to watch a WW2 reenactment of the Japanese attack on Pearl Harbor. It was a huge and realistic production. Japanese Zeros flew over the "harbor" dropping "bombs" and B-17's, B-24's ,B-26's and others scattering into the air to defend our fleet. The brilliant display of pyrotechnics was impressive and moved me deeply. I looked over at my father to see his reaction and saw tears running down his face. It was just too much for him. Our eyes met and he turned and walked away. This was the first time I saw him cry. The memories were too raw.

Acknowledgements

Journal transcription: Jennifer Glassmeyer, Daniel Wickemeyer, Mark Glassmeyer Jr.
Maps designs, and side note copy written by Daniel Wickemeyer.
Introduction written by Jennifer Glassmeyer.
Editing: Kelly Wickemeyer and Kathey Swanson.
This journal contains photos belonging to Edward W. Wickemeyer unless otherwise noted, public domain sources listed below:

Public domain photo sources are noted with these acronyms:

National Archives Catalog	(NAC)
The Naval History and Heritage Command	(NHHC)
Smithsonian Institution Archives	(SIA)
The National WWII Museum	(NWWM)
USGWarchives.com	(USGW)
U.S. Department of Defense	(DOD)

Addresses of Camps Edward stayed at with arrival and departure times...

Recruit Training Detachment
Smyrna Air Base
Base 423
Smyrna, Tennessee

Arrived
Nov. 3, 1942
6.00 o'clock at night

Left
Jan 6, 1943
11:30 o'clock at night

324th Air Base Hdq. Sqd.
Walnut Ridge, Arkansas

Arrived
Jan. 7, 1943
6 o'clock afternoon

Left
Jan 12, 1943
1:45 o'clock afternoon

36th Tech. School Sqd. Base 707
Seymour Johnson Field, North Carolina

Arrived
Jan 14, 1943
9:30 o'clock at night

Left
June 10, 1943
3:30 o'clock afternoon

Class 31 - 43 Squad - 15
A.A.F.T.S. Chevrolet Corp.
2270 E. Jefferson Ave Detroit, Michigan

Arrived
June 12, 1943
8.00 o'clock at night

Left
July 13, 1943
8.00 o'clock at night

1st R & F.O.U. T.C.C Flight D
Baer Field
Ft. Wayne, Indiana

Arrived
July 13, 1943
10 o'clock at night

Left
July 19, 1943
10.20 o'clock at night

87 th T.C.S. 438th T.C.G.
Sedalia Air Base
Warrensburg, Montana

Arrived
July 20, 1943
6:30 o'clock afternoon

Left
July 26, 1943
6 o'clock afternoon

Class C5 - 44 - D T.D. A.A.F.T.T.C.
Douglas Aircraft Co.
Long Beach, California

Arrived
July 29, 1943
12 o'clock afternoon

Left
Sept 1, 1943
1.25 o'clock afternoon

87 th T.C.S. 438th T.C.G.
Sedalia Air Base
Warrensburg, Montana

Arrived
Sept. 4, 1943
8.40 o'clock morning

Left
Oct. 28, 1943
2.20 o'clock afternoon

6th Gunnery Student Sqd
Laredo Air Field Class 44 - 1
Laredo Texas Bks. 551

Arrived
Oct. 31, 1943
2.15 o'clock afternoon

Left
Jan. 5, 1944
3.15 o'clock in morning

Hickam Field
Oahu, Hawaii

Arrived
May 24, 1944
8 o'clock at night

Left
May 27, 1944
10 o'clock morning

Wheeler Field 813th BS. 30th B.G.
Oahu, Hawaii
(A.P.O. 955 c/o P.M. SF, CA)

Arrived
May 27, 1944
10.55 o'clock morning

Left
June 25, 1944
2.30 o'clock afternoon

91st Airborne Sq.
7th AAF Gunnery School
Hickam Field, Hawaii
(A.P.O. 953 - C/O PM SF, CA)

Arrived
June 25, 1944
3.15 o'clock afternoon

Left
July 23, 1944
8.30 o'clock morning

Kuhuku Army Air Base
Oahu Hawaii
(A.P.O. 954 c/o P.M. SF, CA)

Arrived
July 23, 1944
10.00 o'clock Morning

Left
Sept 3rd, 1944
2.00 o'clock Afternoon

Addresses of Camps Continued...

Kwajalein Marshalls
98th Bomb Sq (H) APO 241 11th Bomb Gr.
(c/o P.M. SF. CA.)

Arrived
Sept. 5, 1944
4.30 o'clock afternoon

Left
Oct. 23, 1944
9.40 o'clock morning

Guam Marianas
98th Bomb Sq (H) A.P.O. 246
11th Bomb Gr.
(c/o P.M. SF, CA.)

Arrived
Oct. 23, 1944
6.20 o'clock evening

Left
March 28, 1944
5.45 o'clock Morning

Rest & Recreation Center
Hickam Field, Oahu, Hawaii
A.P.O. 953

Arrived
March 28, 1945
11.30 o'clock morning

Left
April 2, 1945
1.15 o'clock afternoon

Fort Kamhameha
Oahu, Hawaii
A.P.O. 965

Arrived
March 28, 1945
11.30 o'clock morning

Left
April 2, 1945
1.15 o'clock afternoon

Fort Kamehameha Aerial View. (NHHC)

In Closing

In July of 1994, Ed Wickemeyer passed at the age of 72. It wasn't until the summer of 2021 when I was vacationing in Hawaii that I received a call from one of my nephews, Mark Glassmeyer. He seemed very excited and exclaimed, *"You won't believe what mom just found in Grandpa's basement. It's Grandpa's World War II Journal."* We all knew this journal existed, but when asked about it our mother would say, *"Oh yes he wrote it all down but his handwriting was so bad it's hard to read."* We never thought of having it transcribed until Mark called me that day. After our conversation, I thought that publishing his journal as a book would be a fitting reminder of his accomplishments and bravery while recognizing his experiences and sacrifices made during World War II. My hope is this journal will become an heirloom that can be passed down through future generations, fostering a sense of pride, identity, and continuity within our families. Ed's journals provide a unique perspective that textbooks and documentaries may not fully capture.

This is a story of courage, resilience, and sacrifice that I hope can inspire and motivate others. It can encourage us to reflect on our own lives, appreciate the freedoms we enjoy, and develop a greater sense of gratitude and empathy. Memories can fade over time, and important historical details can be lost. By transforming this journal into a book, I hope to ensure that Ed's story is preserved in a tangible and enduring format, safeguarding it from potential loss or deterioration.

Daniel M. Wickemyer

Copyright © 2023 Daniel M. Wickemeyer

All rights reserved. No part of this book may be reproduced in any form or by any electronic of mechanical means, including information storage and retrieval systems, without permission in writing from the author, except by reviewers who may quote brief passages in reviews.

First Edition published by Object8, October 2023.
Books are available in quantity. For information, email dan@object8.com
ISBN: 979-8-9890689-0-6

Edward W. Wickemeyer's war time photo collection can be viewed online at
www.uninvitedb24.com

www.ingramcontent.com/pod-product-compliance
Lightning Source LLC
Chambersburg PA
CBHW041423010526
44119CB00015B/355